Edmund A.P. Hobday

Sketches on Service During the Indian Frontier Campaigns of 1897

Edmund A.P. Hobday

Sketches on Service During the Indian Frontier Campaigns of 1897

ISBN/EAN: 9783337097417

Printed in Europe, USA, Canada, Australia, Japan

Cover: Foto ©ninafisch / pixelio.de

More available books at **www.hansebooks.com**

SKETCHES ON SERVICE DURING THE INDIAN FRONTIER CAMPAIGNS OF 1897

BY

MAJOR E. A. P. HOBDAY, R.A.,

D.A.A.G. 1st Brigade Malakand Field Force.

CONTAINING FIFTY-SEVEN FULL-PAGE ENGRAVINGS FROM ORIGINAL DRAWINGS, AND FOURTEEN PHOTOGRAPHIC PORTRAITS OF THE COMMANDING OFFICERS AND THEIR STAFFS.

LONDON

JAMES BOWDEN, 10, HENRIETTA STREET
COVENT GARDEN, W.C.

1898

PREFACE.

THIS book does not in any way profess to be an historical account of the war. I carried a sketch book with me throughout the operations with which I was fortunate enough to be connected, and made constant use of it, finishing up my rough drawings daily during odd leisure moments in camp, while details were fresh in my mind. In this way I gradually compiled what might be termed a pictorial diary of my wanderings.

The great charm of nearly all the Campaigns of 1897 has been the fact that our troops were operating in hill regions hitherto almost unknown, and never before traversed by any British Force. I can only hope that the pictures of these "new" countries and our doings therein may be of some interest to the general public, in bringing before them some typical scenes of frontier marching and fighting.

I have to thank Sir Bindon Blood, and Generals Elles and Meiklejohn, for much kindness and assistance in enabling me to see so much of the war; also Major Anderson, commanding the 10th Field Battery, R.A., for allowing me to include among these illustrations photographs, taken by him in camp, of the Divisional and Brigade Staffs.

E. A. P. HOBDAY.

RAWAL PINDI,
    January 1st, 1898.

CONTENTS.

FRONTISPIECE: PORTRAIT OF MAJOR-GENERAL SIR BINDON BLOOD.

PREFACE.

INTRODUCTION.

THE SIEGE OF THE MALAKAND AND THE RELIEF OF CHAKDARRA.

	PAGE
PORTRAIT OF COLONEL REID	17
THE FIRST HELIO FROM THE MALAKAND	18
HEAT APOPLEXY CASES AT DARGAI	20
THE MALAKAND, FROM DARGAI	22
CLIMBING THE "ZIG-ZAGS"	24
PORTRAIT OF BRIG.-GENERAL MEIKLEJOHN	27
PICQUET ON THE BUDDHIST ROAD	28
THE SORTIE OF AUGUST 1ST	30
THE SORTIE OF AUGUST 2ND	32
BURNING OF THANNA	34

THE EXPEDITION TO UPPER SWAT.

STAFF OF THE FIRST BRIGADE, MALAKAND FIELD FORCE	39
THE BATTLE OF LANDAKAI	40
GHAZI CHARGE AT LANDAKAI	42
SCENE OF CAVALRY CHARGE NEAR NAWA KILLA	44
"LOOTING" AT GHALEGAI	46
THE SHAMLI PASS	48
UPPER SWAT, FROM THE SHAMLI PASS	50
MANGLAOR	52

CONTENTS.

	PAGE
GUL-I-BAGH	54
SEARCHING FOR HIDDEN GRAIN AT MINGAORA	56
SAIDU AND MOUNT ILM, FROM MINGAORA .	58
BUDDHIST STUPA NEAR GHALEGAI .	60
LOOKING UP THE VALLEY, NEAR GHALEGAI	62
KHAR, LOOKING TOWARDS AMANDARRA .	64

THE MARCH THROUGH BAJOUR.

SIR BINDON BLOOD AND DIVISIONAL STAFF, MALAKAND FIELD FORCE .	69
CHAKDARRA FORT AND BRIDGE .	70
SHGU KU'S GORGE, ON THE PANJKORA RIVER .	72
PANJKORA BRIDGE . . .	74
KHUTTUCK DANCE AT KOTKAI . .	76
JUNCTION OF THE JANDOL AND WATELAI RIVERS .	78
MUNDAH	80
PORTRAIT OF BRIG.-GENERAL JEFFREYS . .	82
RELATIVES OF UMRA KHAN .	83
BARWA	84
LUNCH AT BARWA .	86
JHAR FORT AND MOUNT KOH-I-MOR	88
THE RAMBAT PASS . .	90
VIEW OF THE UTMAN KHEL COUNTRY, FROM THE RAMBAT PASS	92
THE SALARAH PASS . .	94
VIEW NEAR NAWAGAI . .	96
NAWAGAI FORT . . .	98
THE BEDMANAI PASS, FROM NAWAGAI CAMP .	100
MOUNTAIN BATTERY ENTRENCHING	102
STAR SHELL	104
SKIRMISH WITH THE HADDA MULLAH . .	106
PORTRAIT OF BRIG.-GENERAL WODEHOUSE . .	109
THE NIGHT ATTACK AT NAWAGAI. GENERAL WODEHOUSE WOUNDED .	110
MEETING OF GENERALS BLOOD AND ELLES AT LAKARAI	112

CONTENTS.

WITH THE MOHMAND FIELD FORCE.

	PAGE
PORTRAIT OF MAJOR-GENERAL ELLES	117
THE FOOT OF THE BEDMANAI PASS	118
THE FIGHT IN THE BEDMANAI PASS	120
BEDMANAI VILLAGES	122
APPROACH TO THE SHIN DURRA GORGE	124
THE JAROBI VILLAGES	126
FIGHT AT THE HADDA MULLAH'S MOSQUE	128
MANZIRI CHINA	130
THE BOHAI DAG, NEAR THE AFGHAN FRONTIER	132
PORTRAIT OF BRIG.-GENERAL WESTMACOTT	134
PORTRAIT OF MR. MERK, CHIEF POLITICAL OFFICER, MOHMAND FIELD FORCE	135
DESTROYING THE KHUDA KHEL VILLAGES	136
THE SAMGHAKHEI PASS	138
PORTRAIT OF BRIG.-GENERAL MACGREGOR	141
BRIG.-GENERAL MACGREGOR AND STAFF, WITH OFFICERS OF THE 1ST REGT. PATIALA SIKHS	143

BAJOUR ONCE MORE.
AMONG THE MAMUNDS AND SALARZAIS.

STAFF OF THE SECOND BRIGADE, MALAKAND FIELD FORCE	147
INAYAT KILLA	148
DURBAR WITH THE MAMUND JIRGAHS	151
PORTRAIT OF MAJOR DEANE, CHIEF POLITICAL OFFICER, MALAKAND FIELD FORCE	153
MATASHAH	154
PASHAT	156
FORDING THE PANJKORA	158

INTRODUCTION.

In the summer of 1897 I was Station Staff Officer at Rawal Pindi. All through June and July I had had a busy time, as the Tochi Field Force had been organized after the Maizar outrage, and troops and officers had been pouring through Rawal Pindi on their way to Waziristan. At length they had all passed on, and we in Pindi were recovering from the strain and excitement of the few previous weeks, and regretting that it had not been our luck to be sent on service, when the news of the attack on the Malakand came like "a bolt from the blue."

Almost without warning, the clans of the Swat Valley, roused by the fanatical preaching of the so-called "Mad Fakir," attacked the Malakand on the night of the 26th July.

The news was known in India the following day, and on the morning of the 28th came a telegram from Simla, ordering Colonel Reid, 29th Punjab Infantry (who was then officiating as Colonel on the Staff, commanding the troops at Rawal Pindi), to proceed at once to Mardan, taking command of any troops he would find there, and push on as quickly as possible to the relief of the Malakand. As he was directed to nominate his own Staff Officer, I was delighted to learn that he would take me in that capacity. The telegram arrived at 11.30 a.m., and at 1.30 p.m. we were in the train on our way to Nowshera. On our arrival at Nowshera the same evening, we drove on at once to Mardan, by tonga, and arrived there about 10 p.m. We found there the 38th Dogras, who had marched in from Nowshera, and a squadron of the 11th Bengal Lancers, and learned that the 35th Sikhs were also on their way from Peshawur.

The Guides, who are always quartered at Mardan, had made a splendid forced march to the Malakand the previous night, but we found a detachment of their infantry, about 150 strong, consisting of men returned from leave. These, with the Dogras and Lancers, were despatched at 1 a.m. to march to Jalala, the first stage on the road to the Malakand.

Colonel Reid and I remained in Mardan till the 35th Sikhs marched in at 4 a.m., when we set out for Jalala in a tonga to join the troops who had preceded us.

THE SIEGE OF THE MALAKAND
AND
THE RELIEF OF CHAKDARRA.

COLONEL A. I. F. REID, 29TH PUNJAB INFANTRY, COMMANDING THE RELIEF COLUMN TO THE MALAKAND

SIGNALLING BY HELIOGRAPH TO THE MALAKAND FROM JALALA.

EARLY on the morning of the 29th July the little column we had sent off from Mardan reached Jalala, where we joined them about 8 a.m. Communication with the Malakand (some 20 miles off) was now possible by heliograph, and one of the earliest messages received in answer to our enquiries regarding the state of affairs, ran : "Heavy fighting all night. Expect more to-night. What ammunition are you bringing? When may we expect you?" As the situation seemed so serious, Col. Reid sent off Major Beatson, commanding the cavalry, at 10 a.m. to reconnoitre beyond Dargai, our post at the foot of the hills, with instructions to push on if feasible, and reach the Malakand. This he accomplished successfully, and, as the squadron filled all their holsters and haversacks with spare ammunition at Dargai, some 10,000 rounds were thus conveyed to the Malakand garrison.

An attempt was made to push on with the infantry to Dargai at 2 p.m., but the heat was terrible ; men were dropping out fainting by the roadside in twos and threes, an officer's pony fell and died of sunstroke ; so after a few miles Col. Reid called a halt till evening, when the march was continued, and the post reached about 10 p.m.

The officer superintending the signallers in the sketch is Lt. Bailey, the Adjutant of the 38th Dogras, who was afterwards killed in the night attack on Brig.-Genl. Jeffreys' Brigade at Markanai, on the 14th August.

SIGNALLING BY HELIOGRAPH. THE FIRST HELIO FROM THE MALAKAND, JALALA, JULY 29TH, 1897.

HEAT APOPLEXY CASES AT DARGAI.

The 35th Sikhs marched into Dargai at 7.30 a.m. on the 30th. We had left orders for them on the 29th to remain in Mardan during the heat of the day, but in spite of the fact that they marched all night they arrived terribly distressed, and many men were down with heat apoplexy. The scene in the enclosure of the Dargai post was a very sad one, and during the day 19 men of the regiment died.

As the troops were so done up, all we could do on the 30th was to send up the garrison we found at Dargai on marching in—some 200 men. These reached the Malakand safely during the morning. Towards evening bodies of the enemy were seen coming down the hills, and we made all preparations for a night attack. However, we remained unmolested, the only things that happened being a furious dust storm, and some slight showers which cooled the air considerably, but prevented our communicating with the Malakand garrison till about 3 a.m., when we signalled to them by lamp, and learned all was still well there.

HEAT APOPLEXY CASES AT DARGAI, JULY 30TH. 35TH SIKHS.

THE MALAKAND
FROM DARGAI.

At daybreak on the 31st the relief column paraded outside Dargai post. All baggage and stores had been cut down to a minimum, and everything was sacrificed to the carriage of ammunition for the garrison, even the men's great coats being left behind. In this way, with our limited transport, we were enabled to take up 243 mule loads of ammunition, which meant a substantial addition of 291,600 rounds to the supplies of the beleaguered garrison.

We had been advised from the Malakand to avoid both the graded road and the old Buddhist Road, and to push straight up the gorge to the "Zig-zags," the steep track just below the fort; as this, in the event of our advance being opposed, was more thoroughly commanded by the fire of the garrison.

THE MALAKAND, FROM DARGAI.
PARADE OF THE RELIEF COLUMN,
DAYBREAK, JULY 31ST, 1897.

UP THE "ZIG-ZAGS"
TO THE MALAKAND.

The climb up the "Zig-zags," which were reached without opposition, was very hot and trying, and the track was in some places difficult even for mules.

A few of the enemy who came down the gorge from the rocky peaks opposite the Malakand were driven off by volleys from a small flanking party we had sent out to cover the passage of the baggage, under Lt. Vaughan, 35th Sikhs. The climb was over, and all were safely collected on "Gretna Green" about 9.30 a.m.

THE RELIEF COLUMN CLIMBING
THE "ZIG-ZAGS" TO THE
MALAKAND FORT, JULY 31st

BRIGADIER-GENERAL MEIKLEJOHN, C.B., C.M.G., COMMANDING 1st BRIGADE, MALAKAND FIELD FORCE.

PICQUET ON THE BUDDHIST ROAD NEAR CASTLE ROCK.

On arrival in the Malakand, Col. Reid's column were bivouacked temporarily on "Gretna Green," and within a very short time the first casualty occurred, as one of the 38th Dogras had his ankle smashed by a bullet. A dropping fire continued day and night between the picquets and the enemy. Soon after arrival I went with Lt. Gaunt, 4th D.G.'s, Col. Reid's Orderly officer, along the Buddhist Road, to examine the enemy's position from a picquet of the Guides Infantry, who were posted in a "sangar" just beyond a cutting in the cliff through which the road passed. Our appearance on the road was at once greeted with several bullets from the enemy, which came singing overhead from among the boulders on the ridge beyond Castle Rock—a position held throughout the siege by the enemy during the daytime, and from which a constant exchange of shots was carried on with our picquets. The mountain gun on Castle Rock occasionally shelled any large group of the enemy that were seen descending from the crags opposite. This gun belonged to No. 8 Bengal Mountain Battery, and during one of the night attacks on the post, two of the enemy were killed *on* the gun.

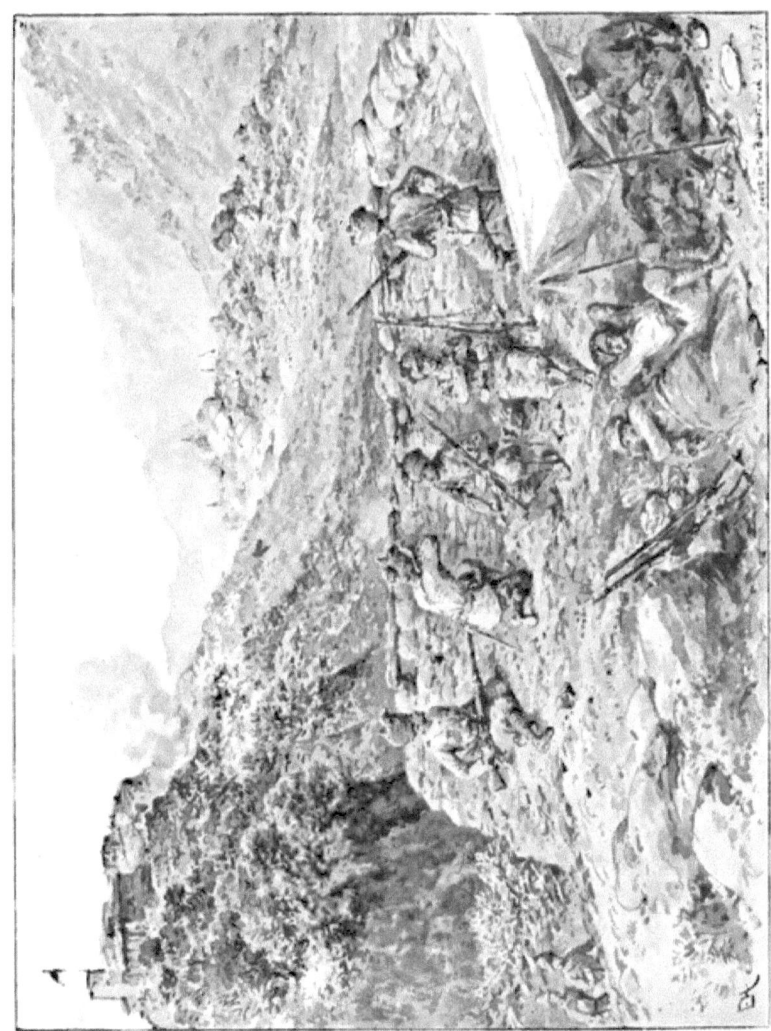

A PICQUET OF THE GUIDES INFANTRY ON THE BUDDHIST ROAD, NEAR CASTLE ROCK. THE MOUNTAIN GUN ON THE FORT SHELLING THE ENEMY.

THE SORTIE OF AUGUST 1st.
11th BENGAL LANCERS AND GUIDES CAVALRY IN ACTION.

On the 1st August an attempt was made to break out and relieve Chakdarra Fort, 10 miles away, which had been hotly attacked ever since the 26th. The 11th Bengal Lancers and Guides Cavalry under Lt.-Col. Adams of the Guides were pushed forward along the road by the old " North Camp," to reconnoitre, while a small column was held in readiness to support them if they succeeded in breaking through. The enemy swarmed down from the hills in great numbers as the cavalry came out, and as the ground beyond North Camp was very bad and full of nullahs, the cavalry were much cramped, and their advance soon checked. A couple of charges were made and the enemy were also held in check by dismounted fire, but masses of them worked along under cover of the nullahs round our flanks. I had brought an order from Col. Meiklejohn to Lt.-Col. Adams to use his discretion according to circumstances, and he now judged it prudent to retire. The cavalry were hard pressed the whole way back, till the enemy came under close fire of the 24th Punjab Infantry, near " Gibraltar " hill. The losses this day were 2 officers of the Guides (Lts. Baldwin and Keyes) wounded, 1 sowar killed and 1 native officer and 10 sowars wounded belonging to the Guides, and 3 sowars of the 11th Bengal Lancers. Lt.-Col. Adams's horse was shot under him, and 5 horses were killed and 22 wounded in the two regiments.

THE SORTIE OF AUGUST 1st.
11th BENGAL LANCERS AND
GUIDES CAVALRY IN ACTION.

THE SORTIE OF AUGUST 2nd, IN SUPPORT OF THE RELIEF OF CHAKDARRA.

THE last signal received from Chakdarra on the morning of the 1st August had been the two words, "Help us," so it was known that the little garrison there were in sore straits. Genl. Sir Bindon Blood arrived at the Malakand on the 1st, and took command from that date. A column under Col. Meiklejohn, who had so ably conducted the defence up to this date, was organised during the afternoon and bivouacked that night on Gretna Green, ready to start at daybreak.

Before daylight on the 2nd a sortie was prepared to support the advance of the relieving column and distract the enemy's attention from it. Accordingly parties of the 35th Sikhs and 38th Dogras under Col. Goldney, 35th Sikhs, assaulted the rocky ridge in front of Castle Rock at dawn. There was very slight opposition, 9 or 10 of the enemy were killed among the rocks and 1 prisoner was taken; the remainder fled. Then the fire of the relieving column was heard as they became hotly engaged on the road to Chakdarra. The smoke of burning villages marked their advance, and from the tower of the fort we saw the cavalry pursuing crowds of the enemy over Khar plain. By midday Chakdarra was relieved, and the enemy, who had besieged it for a week, were dispersing in all directions.

THE NIGHT SORTIE OF AUGUST 1-2, IN SUPPORT OF THE RELIEF OF CHAKDARRA.

THE BURNING
OF THANNA.

THANNA is the largest town in the Swat Valley, and stands on the left bank of the river at the end of a spur almost opposite Chakdarra. After the relief of Chakdarra on 2nd August, Col. Reid moved out from the Malakand on the morning of the 3rd to support Col. Meiklejohn's force, and their united troops under Genl. Sir Bindon Blood proceeded to Alawand and Thanna, which were thoroughly looted and destroyed. Large supplies of grain found there were sent to re-victual Chakdarra Fort. The troops after camping at Thanna for a couple of days, returned a few miles towards the Malakand as far as Amandarra, where a large camp was formed, in which the troops destined to take part in the expedition to Upper Swat were organised and the Brigades formed and told off. Col. Meiklejohn became Brig.-Genl. of the 1st Brigade, and I was appointed his D.A.A.G.

THE BURNING OF THANNA,
AFTER THE RELIEF OF CHAKDARRA.
AUGUST 5TH.

THE EXPEDITION TO UPPER SWAT.

Lieut. Hewett, *Signalling.*
Capt. Dillon, *D.A.Q.M.G.*
Brig.-Gen. Meiklejohn, *C.B., C.M.G.*
Surg. Lt.-Col. D——, *P.M.O.*
Major Hobday, *D.A.A.G.*
Lieut. Duncan, *Asst. Trans. Officer.*
Lieut. Gaunt, *Orderly Officer.*
Capt. Beville, *Brig. Commissariat Officer.*
Capt. Carillon, *Brig. Trans. Officer.*

THE STAFF OF THE 1st BRIGADE, MALAKAND FIELD FORCE.

THE FIGHT AT LANDAKAI.

AFTER remaining some 10 days at Amandarra, and being somewhat delayed by heavy rain, the column for Upper Swat started for Thanna on the afternoon of the 16th August. A reconnaissance that evening up the river showed that the enemy were in force in a strong position on the Landakai Ridge, a spur running down into the river about 5 miles above Thanna. Next morning we moved out to attack them, leaving the baggage and transport animals in camp ready to follow. The 10th Field Battery moved along the river by the road, and came into action with No. 7 Mountain Battery, R.A., just above it, at the foot of a spur about 1,500 yards from the main ridge. The 24th and 31st Punjab Infantry with Genl. Meiklejohn climbed a very steep spur on the right to get above the enemy's main position, taking with them the Native Mountain Battery (No. 8 Bengal). The R. W. Kent supported the artillery, in the rear of whom the cavalry and sappers and miners were formed up. The 45th Sikhs, who had been rear guard, were sent to support Genl. Meiklejohn's attack when they came up. The Landakai Ridge is covered with old Buddhist ruins: some of these on the crest had been converted into a regular fort by the enemy.

A large contingent of Bonerwals began to retire almost before the fight began, and we saw them moving along the top of the hills towards the Morah Pass. This party had a skirmish with the 11th Bengal Lancers guarding the baggage near Thanna.

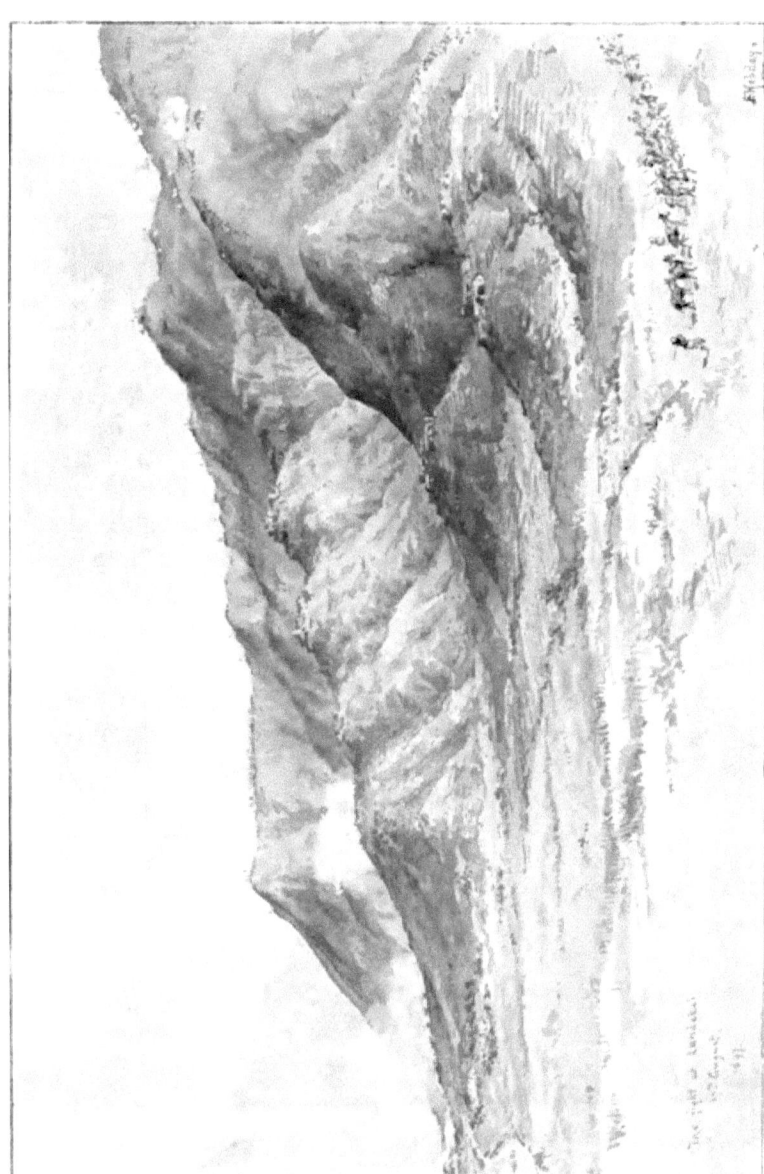

THE FIGHT ON THE
LANDAKAI RIDGE,
AUGUST 17TH

THE GHAZI CHARGE ON THE 24th PUNJAB INFANTRY AT LANDAKAI.

As the main column of attack neared the top of the hill, a hot fire was opened from the enemy's sangars, but it was not very effectual, and only a few men were hit, chiefly by spent bullets. When within about 300 yards of the crest, a halt was called to enable the men to get their breath before the final attack, while No. 8 Mountain Battery shelled the sangars at the top of the hill. Just at this time some half-dozen Ghazis rushed down on the skirmishing line—the Afridi company of the 24th. Nearly all were shot as they came on, but one or two got close up; and one fine young Bonerwal broke right into the front line, driving our Sepoys back some paces before he was shot dead—a very plucky display.

We then pushed on, and the enemy did not wait for us to come to close quarters, but evacuated the sangars, and when we got to the top they were streaming down the rocky nullahs and cliffs on the other side, and across the valley beyond. Many were bagged by volleys, and we then turned to the left, and swept down the ridge towards the "Fort," being joined by four companies of R. W. Kent. When this had been shelled and taken the whole ridge was evacuated, and the enemy were in full flight.

THE GHAZI CHARGE ON THE
24TH PUNJAB INFANTRY
AT LANDAKAI, AUGUST 17TH

NEAR NAWA KILLA, WHERE THE CAVALRY FIGHT TOOK PLACE ON THE 17th AUGUST.

THE causeway at the foot of the Landakai spur had been impracticable for troops, as the enemy had broken it down before the fight. It was now hastily repaired by the Madras Sappers, and the cavalry were enabled to pass it in single file. As we came down the hill after taking the ridge, the cavalry began to appear in twos and threes round the spur; but the enemy, whom we had been shelling as they fled across the valley, had a good start and were now close to the foot of the opposite hills, and were beginning to collect on a spur above Nawa Killa. As the cavalry strung out they only arrived in very small numbers, and the officers, being better mounted, forged ahead of their men. As they got up to Nawa Killa a tremendously heavy fire was opened from the hill sides, and Capt. Palmer, who was leading, had his horse shot, and was hit through the wrist after cutting down a standard bearer at the foot of the hill. Lt. Greaves was wounded and cut up by swordsmen almost immediately after, and his body was saved by Col. Adams and Lord Fincastle. Lt. McLean of the Guides had taken his men under cover of some trees, and opened fire on the hill. He now ran out to help the others bring in Greaves's body, but was shot through both thighs, and died in a few minutes from loss of blood. When we got up the enemy had retired to the top of the hills, where we shelled them till they were out of sight. A few were caught and bayonetted by a party of the 31st Punjab Infantry.

NEAR NAWA KILLA. THE SCENE OF THE CAVALRY FIGHT OF AUGUST 17TH, WHEN LIEUTS. McLEAN AND GREAVES WERE KILLED.

LOOTING AT GHALEGAI, AUGUST 18th.

AFTER the fight the force gradually re-assembled (with the exception of the 10th Field Battery, which returned to Thanna), and formed an entrenched bivouac between the villages of Landakai and Kotah. The baggage now began to arrive, but owing to the difficulties of the narrow track below the cliffs overhanging the river, it did not all get in till 10 o'clock at night. On the following day, the 18th, we marched to Ghalegai, which was also looted. As our force had only two days' grain for animals at starting, we systematically searched all villages for grain to supply their wants. In Ghalegai a good deal of Government property, such as saddles, tents, ropes, &c., were found, which had been captured by the enemy when the North Camp was evacuated at Malakand. Among the household gods of the natives were some rather choice old handwritten Korans, many of which were annexed as "reminiscences" by the officers of the force. The followers and troops fared sumptuously in the matter of fowls, which must now be scarce in the Swat Valley.

LOOTING AT GHALEGAI,
UPPER SWAT VALLEY
AUGUST 18th

THE SHAMLI PASS, NEAR MINGAORA.

The day following the march to Ghalegai we reached Mingaora, a large town in Upper Swat, where we remained until the 24th. On the 21st a reconnaissance was made higher up the valley by the Guides Cavalry, two companies 24th Punjab Infantry, and two guns No. 7 Mountain Battery. The spur beyond Mingaora runs into the Swat River, and there is no road round it by the bank, so the reconnaissance had to move up the valley and cross it by a very steep and rough track known as the Shamli Pass. Going up there was only a narrow track covered with loose boulders, while the descent on the other side was even worse, down a torrent bed with huge rocks and steep ledges, along which the horses had to scramble as best they could.

THE SHAMLI PASS,
NEAR MINGAORA.

VIEW OF THE UPPER SWAT VALLEY FROM THE TOP OF THE SHAMLI PASS.

THE view from the top of the pass was very fine. The Swat River runs through a very fertile tract of country, the low lying ground being one mass of rice fields, while the upper slopes were covered with fields of Indian corn. There are several large valleys which join the main valley, the high hills behind stretching away to Kohistan.

After descending the ravine we halted near a fine stretch of olive groves beyond the village of Charuji, and under a round hillock which had evidently been surmounted at one time by some Buddhist buildings.

VIEW OF THE UPPER SWAT VALLEY, FROM THE TOP OF THE SHAMLI PASS.

MANGLAOR.

BEYOND the olive groves was a stream where we watered our horses. This runs down from the valley, at the mouth of which is Manglaor, another large village. This is mentioned in ancient history as being a thriving town in the Buddhist period, and there are many ruins and caves and other signs of the Buddhist occupation near it. The Kotke Pass leads from the Manglaor nullah over the hills towards the Indus.

Leaving the infantry and guns near Manglaor, the cavalry pushed on up the Swat Valley. After the rain of the night before, the going was very heavy, and some of the tracks across the rice fields were almost impassable.

MANGLAOR. THE CAVALRY ADVANCE ALONG THE UPPER SWAT VALLEY, AUGUST 22ND.

GUL-I-BAGH.

The spur above Gul-i-Bagh was the farthest point reached by the cavalry on the 21st, and the most distant point in the Swat Valley visited during the expedition.

No opposition of any kind was experienced, and at Gul-i-Bagh the villagers came out and voluntarily offered to surrender their arms and standards. These latter were taken back with us, but we could not convey the arms, so the people were told to bring them into Mingaora.

A reservist of the Guides was found living in the village. The stout gentleman with the thick legs in the sketch acted as our guide on this day. He declared he was eighty years old, and had been at Delhi with Nicholson!—whether this were true or not, he certainly spoke excellent Hindustani.

A thunderstorm, which swept across from the hills on the opposite side of the river, caught us and drenched us thoroughly. We got a view of the snows of Kohistan, which was very fine. It was hoped that we should not have to retrace our steps over the Shamli Pass, but our patrols reported that there was absolutely no track round by the river bed, so there was nothing for it but to face the pass once more; so the trying scramble among boulders and ravines was gone through again, and we eventually reached camp without further mishap than the loss of many horseshoes and a few rolls and tumbles among the rocks.

GUL-I-BAGH, AND THE UPPER SWAT VALLEY. THE FARTHEST POINT REACHED BY THE EXPEDITION.

SEARCHING FOR HIDDEN GRAIN AT MINGAORA.

WHILE we were at Mingaora, the usual searching parties were organized to find grain for the animals. The inhabitants had buried a good deal, and on one occasion a rather amusing episode occurred in connection with one of these hidden stores. At the entrance to one of the houses we found an old man lying on a mat, groaning, and apparently terribly ill. However, we entered and searched the house, but without finding any supplies. As we were leaving the court-yard, Capt. Beville, our commissariat officer, sank above the ankles into a soft bit of ground; so we brought in a few Madras Sappers who accompanied the search parties, and they soon brought to light a large amount of grain cunningly stored in big copper cauldrons, and buried with a collection of agricultural tools and household gods of sorts. When the "sick man" found his store had been unearthed, he recovered in the most miraculous manner, and, hopping up from his mat, started abusing us all most heartily.

SEARCHING FOR HIDDEN GRAIN AT MINGAORA.

SAIDU AND MOUNT ILM, FROM OUR CAMP AT MINGAORA.

OPPOSITE our camp at Mingaora, on the other side of the stream running down from the Kalel Pass, was the village of Saidu, where the old Akhund of Swat is buried. His tomb is now a shrine of pilgrimage, and one of the holiest places in the Swat Valley. During our stay at Mingaora, Mussulman Sepoys were allowed on one day to visit the shrine, but no one else was permitted to go near the place.

The large hill in the distance in the sketch is Mount Ilm, which overlooks Boner. We were in camp at Mingaora from the 19th to the 24th August.

SAIDU AND MOUNT ILM.
FROM THE CAMP AT MINGAORA.

BUDDHIST STUPA AT SHANKARDAR, NEAR GHALEGAI.

On the 24th August we marched back from Mingaora to Burikot. Between Ghalegai and Burikot, near a small village called Shankardar, is a very fine old Buddhist "Stupa," in excellent preservation. It has evidently been dug into frequently to search for treasure, but one side is nearly intact, and the stone-work fairly well preserved.

There are other similar stupas in many parts of the valley, notably near Burikot, towards the Karikar Pass, but the one in the sketch was the finest we saw, and certainly the most complete.

BUDDHIST STUPA AT SHANKARDAR, NEAR GHALEGAI.

LOOKING UP THE VALLEY, NEAR GHALEGAI.

BETWEEN Ghalegai and Burikot the track runs at the foot of some fine cliffs, and is probably the remnant of an old Buddhist road, as it is paved in many places with large stone slabs. A very fine view of the snows was obtained looking up the valley from the spot where we breakfasted on this march.

The group sitting among the rocks shows Genl. Meiklejohn on the right; Capt. Dillon, D.A.Q.M.G., above him; Lt. Gaunt, Orderly officer, leaning against a stone; and myself sketching, seated on another. The old native officer is a fine old retired Afridi Subadar-Major of the 20th Punjab Infantry, named Zeman Khan, who voluntarily came and joined his old commanding officer, Genl. Meiklejohn, during the siege of the Malakand, and remained with him as extra Orderly officer during the Swat campaign, doing very good and faithful service.

No. 8 Bengal Mountain Battery, under Capt. Birch, R.A., is passing in the foreground of the sketch.

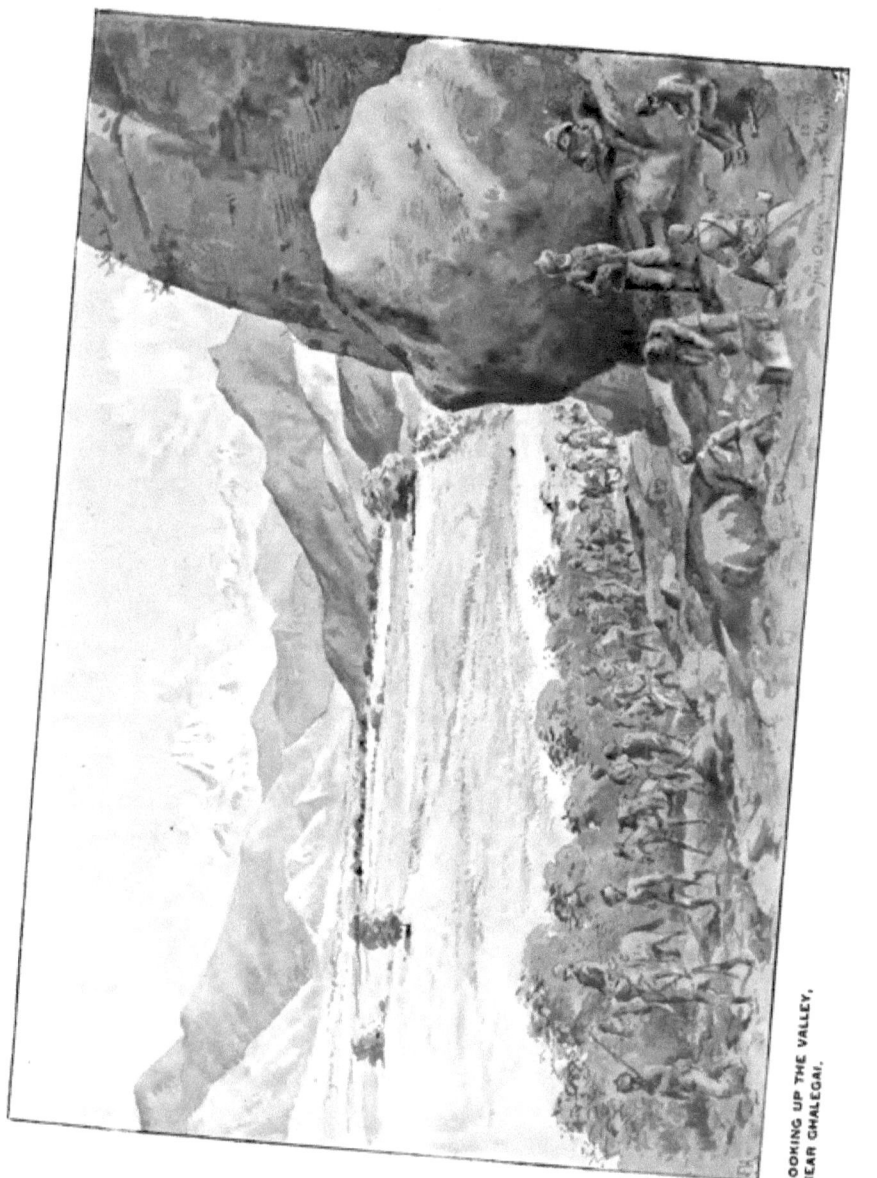

LOOKING UP THE VALLEY, NEAR GHALEGAI.

KHAR, LOOKING TOWARDS AMANDARRA.

THE 1st Brigade were back at Thanna on the 26th August, after their tour in Upper Swat, and on the 27th marched to Khar, where they relieved the 2nd Brigade.

We stayed at Khar a long time, guarding the commissariat and ordnance depôts; while the 2nd Brigade made some small tours into the Utman Khel country, and the 3rd Brigade came up from Rustam, and went on towards the Panjkora.

At one time, on the 4th September, nearly the whole of the Malakand Field Force was collected at Khar, the Brigades being complete except the 3rd, which had not all its regiments present.

KHAR, LOOKING TOWARDS AMANDARRA. ENCAMPMENT OF THE THREE BRIGADES OF THE MALAKAND FIELD FORCE.

THE MARCH THROUGH BAJOUR.

Major BLUNT,
Field Engineer.

Lt.-Col. MEIKLEJOHN,
A.Q.M.G.

Capt. EDWARDES,
Prov. Marshal.

Vet. Capt. MANN,
Sen. Vet. Officer.

Gen. SIR BINDON BLOOD,
K.C.B.

Capt. DICK,
Orderly Officer.

Major BICKNEY,
A.A.G.

Lt.-Col. ASTWELL, C.B.,
C.R.A.

Lord FINCASTLE,
Orderly Officer.

The Rev. E. KETON,
Chaplain.

Capt. LYE,
Intel. L.G.O.

Capt. HENDERSON, R.E.,
Survey Officer.

Capt. STANTON, D.S.O.,
*D.A.Q.M.G.,
Intell. Branch.*

Capt. PLINKETT,
Aed. to the Trans. Officer.

Capt. BYNDEVILLE,
A.D.C.

Capt. NORIE,
Supt. Army Signalling.

Major WILMOT,
Chief Commt. Officer.
Capt. TILACKWELL,
Dist. Trans. Officer.

MAJOR-GENERAL SIR BINDON BLOOD, K.C.B., COMMANDING MALAKAND FIELD FORCE, AND OFFICERS OF DIVISIONAL STAFF.

CHAKDARRA FORT AND BRIDGE.

THE expedition against the Mohmands had now begun, and the 2nd and 3rd Brigades of the Malakand Field Force were ordered up to Bajour. My Brigade, the 1st, was left on the line of communications, but Genl. Sir Bindon Blood attached me to his Staff on special duty; so I was enabled to accompany him throughout the operations that now began, and left Khar to join him on the 7th September. Chakdarra Fort commands the bridge built across the Swat River during the Chitral campaign, and was besieged, like the Malakand, from the 26th July to the 2nd August, when it was relieved by Col. Meiklejohn's column.

I was unable to show one of the chief features of the place in the sketch for want of space, *i.e.*, the hill on which the Signal Tower stands, which comes down close to the left hand corner of the Fort in the picture. It was the fire from this hill that was so dangerous during the siege.

CHAKDARRA FORT AND THE
BRIDGE ACROSS THE SWAT RIVER.

THE SHIGU KUS GORGE ON THE PANJKORA RIVER.

BEYOND Chakdarra the road runs over the Katgola Pass to Serai, where the 2nd Brigade encamped on the 7th September. From this the country drops down to the Panjkora River, and the road strikes the stream where it turns off to join the Swat River, through a wild gorge in the hills called the Shigu Kus, shut in by high cliffs, through which the river rushes in a succession of rapids and whirlpools.

THE SHIGU KUS GORGE ON THE PANJKORA RIVER.

THE PANJKORA
BRIDGE.

THE 3rd Brigade, under General Wodehouse, had been pushed on ahead, and had saved the Panjkora Suspension Bridge from being interfered with by the Bajouris. They were encamped by the river on the 8th September, when the 2nd Brigade crossed, and the sketch was made from the 10th Field Battery position, on a knoll overlooking the stream.

The bridge was built in 1895, during the Chitral campaign, and the Khan of Dir has since been responsible for its safety.

THE PANJKORA SUSPENSION BRIDGE. SECOND BRIGADE CROSSING.

KHUTTUCK DANCE BY THE GUIDES AT KOTKAI.

THE 2nd Brigade encamped at Kotkai, about two miles beyond the Panjkora Bridge, on the 8th September. While waiting for the baggage to come up, some of the Afridis of the Guides Infantry started a "Khuttuck dance" to the strains of a "dōl," or Afghan drum, and some "surnais," as the pipes of the country are termed. In spite of their just having marched some 15 miles, the dancers whirled away with great energy for about an hour, till the arrival of the transport.

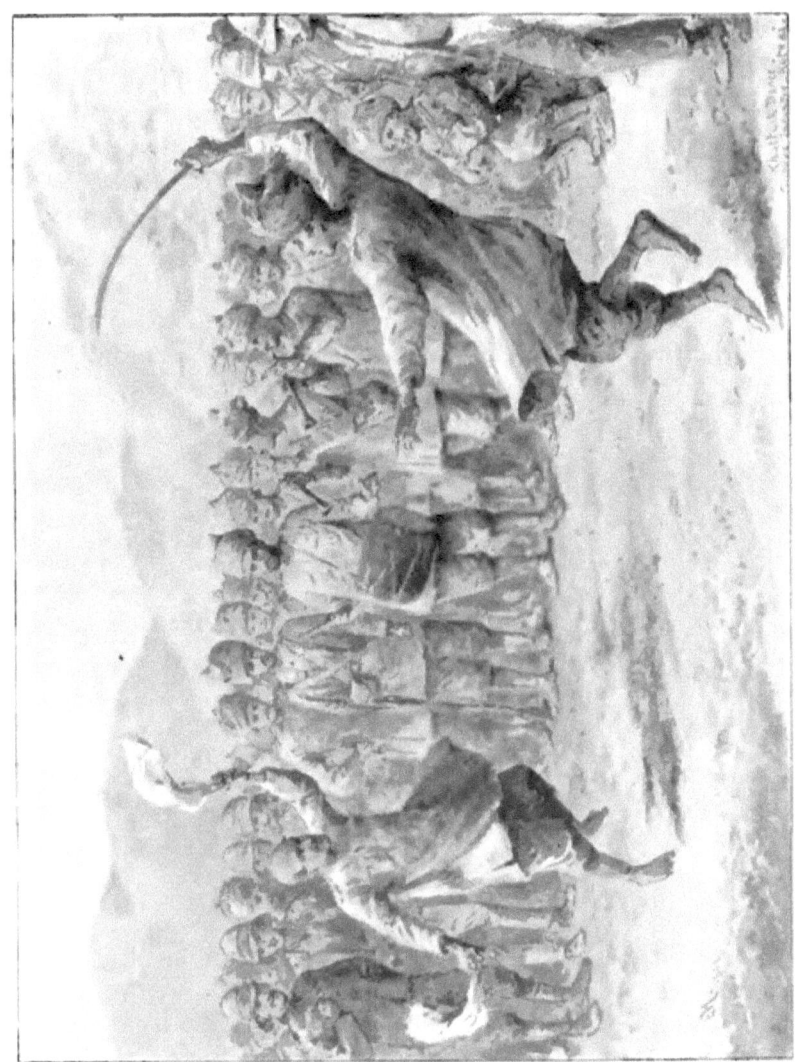

KHUTTUCK DANCE BY THE
GUIDES INFANTRY AT KOTKAI.

THE JUNCTION OF THE JANDOL AND WATELAI RIVERS.

GHOSAM was a camp about six miles beyond Kotkai, where the 2nd Brigade remained for a couple of days, at the entrance of the Jandol Valley, close to Mundah Fort. The 3rd Brigade here passed the 2nd, and took the lead, camping some four miles further west near Shakrata. The valleys here were full of feathery waving grass, besides the usual rice crops, and there were some fine views up the valleys towards the Janbatai Pass, and in the direction of Nawagai.

THE JUNCTION OF THE JANDOL AND WATELAI RIVERS, LOOKING TOWARDS NAWAGAI FROM

MUNDAH.

Mundah Fort was well known during the Chitral campaign, and our forces were then encamped for some months round it. Umra Khan brought Lieuts. Fowler and Edwards to this fort after he took them prisoners, and sent them over the hills to the British camp, which was then at Sado on the Panjkora.

The sketch was taken from the "Buffs'" camp on the opposite bank of the Jandol River to Mundah.

MUNDAH, FROM THE "BUFFS'"
CAMP ON THE JANDOL RIVER.

BRIG.-GENERAL JEFFREYS, C.B.,
COMMANDING 2ND BRIGADE,
MALAKAND FIELD FORCE.

BARWA.

On the 10th September two squadrons of the 11th Bengal Lancers under Major Beatson went out with Major Deane, the Political Officer, up the Jandol Valley as far as Barwa. We went to visit sundry refractory Khans, notably at Tor, a fort between Mundah and Barwa. On arrival at Barwa we inspected the fort, which was Umra Khan's favourite stronghold. It is of the ordinary type of Afghan fort, but a superior specimen, as there was some pretension to architecture in the way of carved balconies and window shutters, &c.

From the large square tower Umra Khan shot one of his brothers, with whom he had a quarrel.

BARWA (UMRA KHAN'S FAVOURITE STRONGHOLD) AND THE JANBATAI PASS.

LUNCH AT BARWA.

At Barwa we spent the heat of the day in a lovely chenar grove by a spring, just below the Fort; and here we were entertained by the Khan, who had charpoys covered with carpets and rugs set out for us, and soon strings of retainers appeared with bowls and baskets containing all manner of refreshments—rice, pillaus, curry, stewed kids, baked fowls, Afghan bread (very different from the ordinary chupattie), grapes, apples, and all kinds of good things. We graciously accepted a share of these, and the remainder were handed over to the escort, of whom the Mussulmans fared sumptuously!

The members of the party besides myself on this occasion were :—Major Deane, Political Officer ; Major Beatson, Major Delamain, Lt. Waterfield, 11th Bengal Lancers ; Lord Fincastle, 16th Lancers ; and Lt. Churchill, 4th Hussars. Needless to say we took all precautions against a repetition of the Maizar affair.

LUNCH AT BARWA, SEPT. 9TH.
UMRA KHAN'S BROTHER,
MAHOMED SHAH KHAN, SENDS
REFRESHMENTS.

JHAR FORT AND MOUNT KOH-I-MOR.

Sir Bindon Blood now pushed on towards Nawagai with Genl. Wodehouse's Brigade, the 2nd Brigade under Genl. Jeffreys following a day's march in rear.

Jhar was passed on the morning of the 12th, *en route* to our camp near Shum-Shuk, beyond Khar. The Khans of both Jhar and Khar were friendly throughout the operations, and did good service.

Koh-i-mor, the large hill in the background, is a great landmark in the Nawagai Valley. It lies in the Utman Khel country on the right bank of the Watelai River, south of Bajour.

JHAR FORT, NAWAGAI, AND MOUNT KOH-I-MOR.

APPROACH TO THE RAMBAT PASS.

From our camp near Shum-Shuk Sir Bindon Blood reconnoitred the Rambat Pass, which leads through the Utman Khel country to the Ambahar Valley in the Mohmand country.

The pass is not a difficult one for mules, and the gradient fairly easy. The village near the pass had been deserted when we visited it, and the inhabitants were encamped on the top of the surrounding hills, but seemed inclined to be hostile.

APPROACH TO THE RAMBAT PASS,
LEADING THROUGH THE
UTMAN KHEL COUNTRY TO THE
MOHMAND COUNTRY.

VIEW OF THE UTMAN KHEL COUNTRY FROM THE TOP OF THE RAMBAT PASS.

THERE is a steep descent from the Rambat Pass towards the Ambahar Valley, and the country below is much more arid and waterless than the Nawagai country above.

The 2nd Brigade were to have moved into the Mohmand country by this pass, but were attacked in their camp on the north side of the pass on the night of the 14th, and, owing to the necessity for punishing the Mamunds who made this attack the whole plan of operations was changed, and the 2nd Brigade remained to fight the Mamunds in Bajour.

VIEW OF THE UTMAN KHEL (MOHMAND) COUNTRY FROM THE TOP OF THE RAMBAT PASS

THE SALARAH PASS.

BEYOND the Rambat, in the direction of Nawagai, is a very easy pass, the Salarah, leading into the same valley as the Rambat. The Nawagai Valley is here much cut up with enormous ravines. The country between these is quite level, so that at a distance they are not visible and the whole valley looks like a flat plain, and the chief village is named from this fact Loe-sam—the big plain.

THE SALARAH PASS

LOOKING EAST FROM THE HEAD OF THE NAWAGAI VALLEY.

At the head of the Nawagai Valley the watershed is almost imperceptible. The track comes up out of one ravine, and gradually drops down into another running in the opposite direction round the spur on which Nawagai Fort is built.

The scene looking back down the valley of the Watelai from this slight rise is very fine, and one gets a good comprehensive view of Koh-i-mor and the various passes leading south.

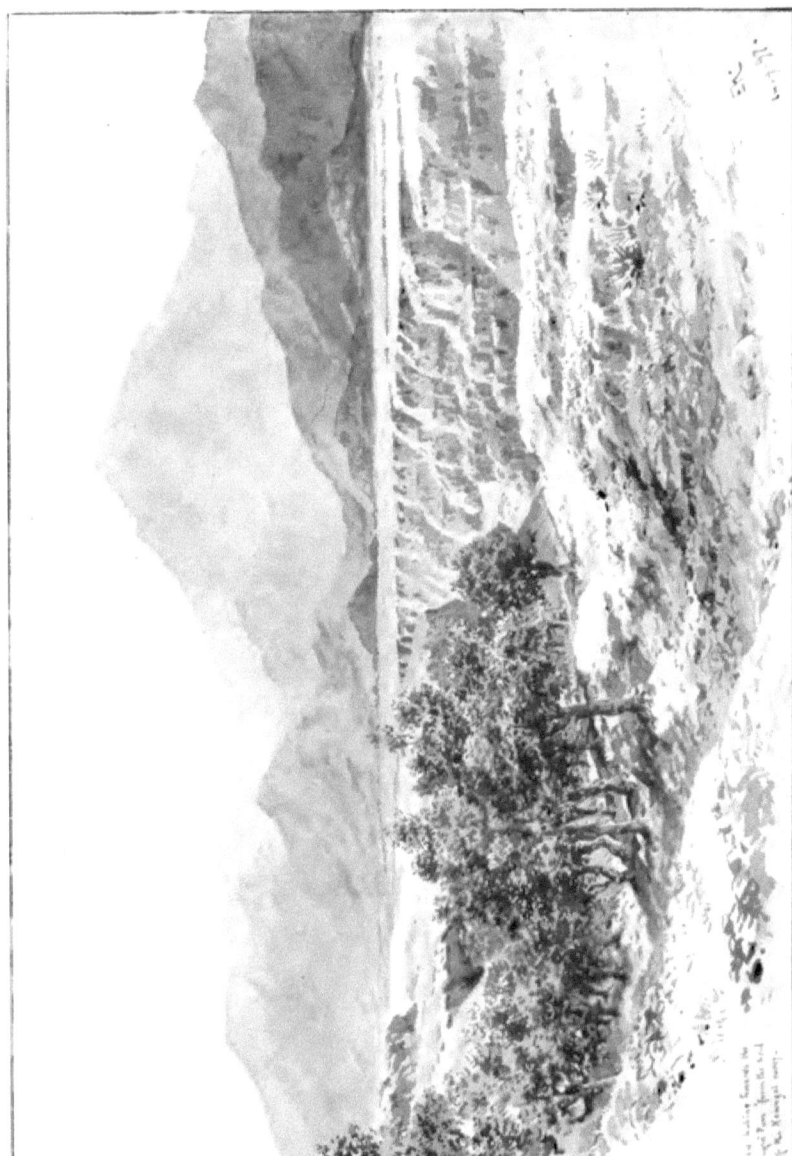

LOOKING EAST FROM THE HEAD
OF THE NAWAGAI VALLEY,
TOWARDS THE INZIRI PASS.

NAWAGAI FORT.

The Khan of Nawagai's Fort stands on a steep rocky spur overlooking a picturesque ravine that opens out on to the Mittai Valley. At the entrance of this open plain the 3rd Brigade encamped—about half a mile from Nawagai itself.

NAWAGAI FORT AND VILLAGE.

THE BEDMANAI PASS FROM NAWAGAI CAMP.

THE 3rd Brigade with the Divisional Headquarter's Staff now sat at Nawagai for a week, waiting for the arrival of the Mohmand Field Force, which was on its way up from Shubkudder, commanded by General Elles. The Hadda Mullah's " Lushkar " was collected in the villages at the foot of the Bedmanai Pass and the Mittai Valley, and increased daily. Cavalry reconnaissances were made in all directions, chiefly to open communication with General Elles's force, which was delayed on its way up by the difficulties of the road among the lower hills south of the Nahaki Pass.

THE BEDMANAI PASS, FROM THE CAMP AT NAWAGAI, SEPTEMBER 17TH.

No. 1 MOUNTAIN BATTERY ENTRENCHING THE CAMP AT NAWAGAI.

During the halt at Nawagai the camp was well entrenched. No. 1 Mountain Battery, R.A., under Major Norton, were on the face of the camp fronting the Bedmanai Pass.

The figures on the right of the sketch are Sepoys of the 22nd Punjab Infantry and 39th Garhwalis, the two native regiments of the 3rd Brigade.

No. 1 MOUNTAIN BATTERY ENTRENCHING THE CAMP AT NAWAGAI, SEPTEMBER 19TH.

STAR SHELL, ON THE NIGHT OF THE 19th SEPTEMBER.

On the night of the 19th September occurred what was known afterwards as the " Little " night attack. We had been warned by the Nawagai " friendlies " that an attack was contemplated, and they had arranged to light a signal fire at the foot of a spur opposite camp, if the enemy were coming across the plain. The fire was lighted about 9.30 p.m., and firing began soon afterwards from the hill near, and, later, on the west and south faces of the camp. There was a good deal of shouting, but the enemy never tried a regular rush, and after an hour or so of pretty heavy firing all round on both sides, the attack died away. We had a few casualties.

The sketch was taken at the end of the Staff " street " near Sir Bindon Blood's tent, and his escort of Guides Infantry are shown turned out with fixed bayonets. Star shell was being fired over the plain by No. 1 Mountain Battery.

NIGHT ATTACK AT NAWAGAI,
SEPTEMBER 19TH. No. 1 MOUNTAIN
BATTERY, R.A., FIRING STAR SHELL.

SKIRMISH WITH THE HADDA MULLAH.

On two or three occasions the Hadda Mullah's army came out and gathered in the open ground at the foot of the Bedmanai Pass, some six or seven miles off. This used generally to happen late in the afternoon, and seemed more of the nature of a parade than any offensive move. The cavalry used to go out and skirmish with outlying parties, and part of the Brigade would march two or three miles out from camp, and generally send a few shots at long range from the Mountain Battery; but as the enemy did not come on, it was too late to follow him up so far from camp, and both sides usually returned to their respective bivouacs at dusk.

On the 20th, however, the enemy were seen to be following us up in the distance as we retired, and so a night attack was prepared for, which duly came off. Genl. Elles was expected to arrive within reach next day, and the Hadda Mullah had seemingly determined to try and crush the 3rd Brigade before Genl. Elles's arrival.

A SKIRMISH WITH THE HADDA MULLAH AT THE FOOT OF THE BEDMANAI PASS.

BRIG.-GENERAL WODEHOUSE
C.B., C.M.G., COMMANDING
3RD BRIGADE, MALAKAND
FIELD FORCE.

THE NIGHT ATTACK AT NAWAGAI ON THE 20th SEPTEMBER. GENERAL WODEHOUSE WOUNDED.

THE Hadda Mullah's force must have got silently into position and remained ready for some signal, which was anticipated by our lighting bonfires in front of the south face of the camp, as previously arranged, at 9 p.m. On the first fire being lighted, a heavy discharge of musketry opened from three sides of the camp from every bit of rising ground and cover within reach. Tents were struck at once, and volleys and star shell began, with occasional rounds of case by the battery into the nullah, where the enemy's swordsmen collected for their rushes. From 9 p.m. till 2.30 a.m. the firing was almost incessant all round, and there were constant charges on three faces of the camp by swordsmen, more especially at the south-west corner, where the Queen's were posted, and where the enemy must have suffered heavily from the Dum-Dum bullet. About 12 o'clock Genl Wodehouse was hit while walking back from reporting to Genl. Blood—about ten yards off where I was sitting. The hospital tents were hit over and over again, and the Staff "street" seemed a special mark for the enemy's riflemen; probably the tents lying on the ground gave them a capital line to aim at.

The enemy had plenty of Martinis and a few Lee-Metfords, whose sound could easily be distinguished, and the ammunition of which was found in one or two places next day. At about 1 a.m. there was a slight lull; but a furious attack followed, which proved to be the last. This, we heard afterwards, was caused by the enemy beginning to retire, but on finding that a certain Khan of some note had been left dead in front of the entrenchment, a final attack was made to recover his body. When the moon rose the firing ceased, but there was little light then, and previously it had been pitch dark. Our losses were 1 man killed and about 30 wounded. The animals suffered heavily, 44 being killed and 89 wounded, including a large number of officers' chargers and cavalry horses. Next morning 7 or 8 bodies were lying close to the entrenchment, and some 15 or 20 others were found hastily buried close by. We heard subsequently that the enemy lost over 300.

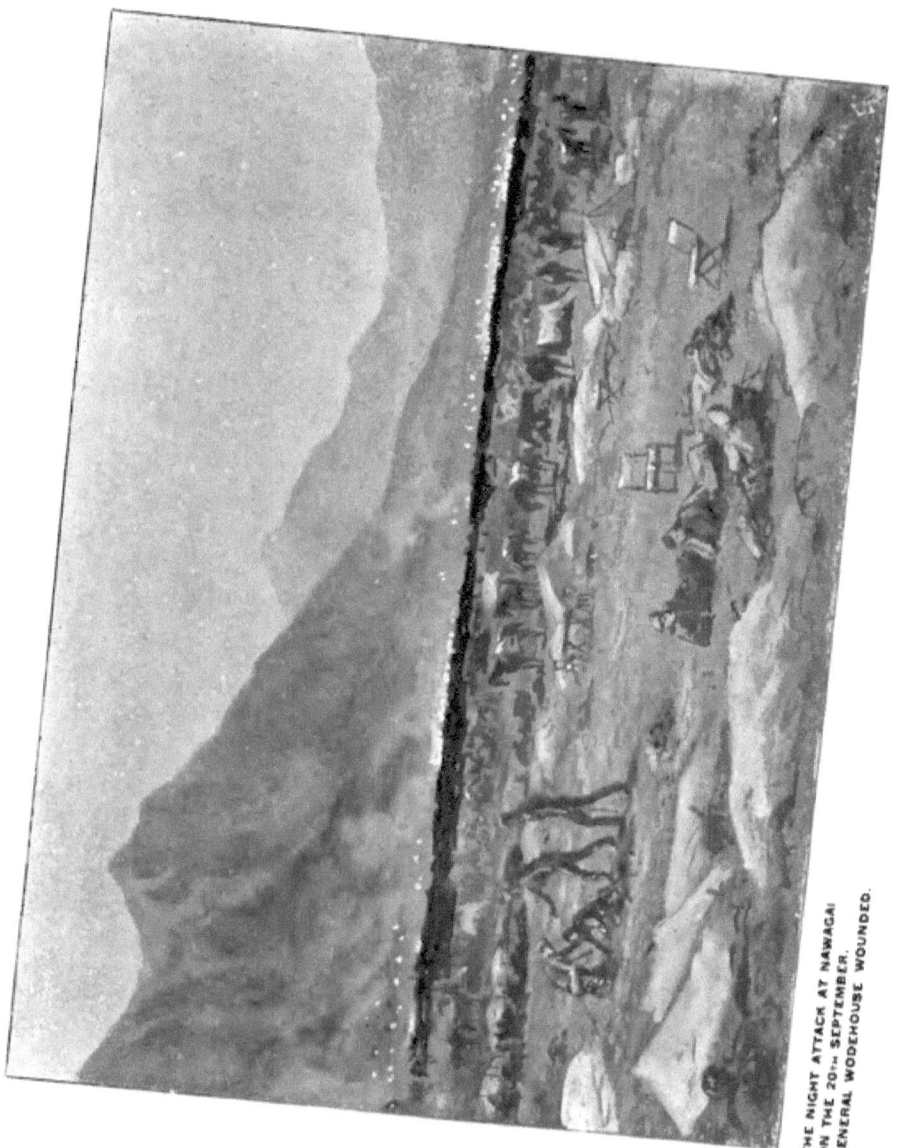

THE NIGHT ATTACK AT NAWAGAI
ON THE 20TH SEPTEMBER.
GENERAL WODEHOUSE WOUNDED.

THE MEETING OF GENERALS
BLOOD AND ELLES
AT LAKARAI.

The morning after the attack Sir Bindon Blood rode out to Lakarai about six miles off, and met Genl. Elles, who was marching up with his 1st Brigade (Genl. Westmacott's).

The news of the Tirah appointments had now arrived, and I found that Genl. Meiklejohn had been appointed with his whole Staff to the 2nd Brigade, 1st Division. Sir Bindon Blood gave me permission to accompany Genl. Elles's force through the Mohmand country, and rejoin my Brigade Staff at Peshawur, as this was a shorter route than having to go all the way back through Bajour and Malakand, and Genl. Meiklejohn was then on the other side of the Panjkora River. So I had the good fortune to see the end of the operations against the Hadda Mullah, and another new country!

THE MEETING OF GENERAL SIR BINDON BLOOD AND GENERAL ELLES AT LAKARAI, SEPT. 21ST.

WITH THE MOHMAND FIELD FORCE.

MAJOR-GENERAL ELLES, C.B.,
COMMANDING THE MOHMAND
FIELD FORCE.

THE FOOT OF THE BEDMANAI PASS.

The 3rd Brigade Malakand Field Force was now attached to Genl. Elles's force, and joined them in camp at Kuz Chinari, at the entrance of the Bedmanai Pass, on the 22nd; Sir Bindon Blood having gone back with the 11th Bengal Lancers to join Genl. Jeffreys' Brigade in Bajour, which had been having severe fighting.

The Bedmanai Pass was attacked on the 23rd September and captured with small opposition, as the greater portion of the Hadda Mullah's army had dispersed after the night attack, and gone up the Mittai Valley over the border into Asmar.

Bar Chinari village is at the foot of the ascent, where the track winds up a long nullah to the pass.

The 20th Punjab Infantry and 2nd/1st Gurkhas crowned the hills on the left of the sketch, and the 2nd Queen's (Royal West Surrey) and Garhwalis took the hills on the right, the remainder of the two Brigades moving up the valley.

The cavalry had a skirmish up the Mittai Valley with some scattered parties.

THE FOOT OF THE
BEDMANAI PASS, FROM
BAR CHINARI VILLAGE

THE FIGHT IN THE BEDMANAI PASS.

On the high hills in the left of the sketch were a few sangars, which were captured by the 20th Punjab Infantry and Gurkhas. No. 3 Mountain Battery (under Lt.-Col. Dacres Cunningham) and a Maxim gun also operated on these hills. About half way up the valley No. 1 Mountain Battery and No. 5 Bombay Mountain Battery also came into action against bodies of the enemy retiring over the pass and up the heights on the right.

When the crest of the pass was reached, the 3rd Brigade Malakand Field Force was sent back to operate in the Mittai Valley, while the 1st Brigade Mohmand Field Force crossed the Kotal and seized the group of Bedmanai villages about a mile beyond, in which they bivouacked for the night, after getting all their transport over the pass—a long business.

There were only some 8 or 10 casualties on this day, and the opposition was very feeble; probably not more than 500 of the enemy, all told, were present.

THE FIGHT IN THE BEDMANAI PASS, SEPTEMBER 23RD.

BEDMANAI AND VILLAGES, FROM THE TOP OF THE PASS.

The Bedmanai villages were a cluster of strongly fortified hamlets in the basin between the Bedmanai and Torakhwa Passes. The Brigade bivouacked in them on the night of the 23rd September, and when we moved on the following day to Torakhwa, all the towers were blown up and the villages burnt.

BEDMANAI AND VILLAGES, FROM THE TOP OF THE PASS.

APPROACH TO THE
SHIN DURRA GORGE.

Jarobi, which was known to be the Hadda Mullah's stronghold, was the next objective, and, after leaving Torakhwa, the force marched up the Bohai Dag on the 25th. The Mohmand Valley is a bare stony plain without a green thing on it, except some coarse grass. The whereabouts of Jarobi was very imperfectly known, and our guides brought us at last to the entrance of a gorge called the Shin Durra, in which they said it lay.

The figure with the spear among the Staff in the sketch is the Maharajah of Patiala. He and his Staff always carried hog-spears. One of his Imperial Service Regiments was at this time with the 3rd Brigade Malakand Field Force in the Mittai Valley.

Moghul Khor, the village near the entrance of the pass, was destroyed, as some shots were fired from the hills above. No. 3 Mountain Battery fired a few rounds, and the heights were crowned by the 2nd/1st Gurkhas on the left and 20th Punjab Infantry on the right.

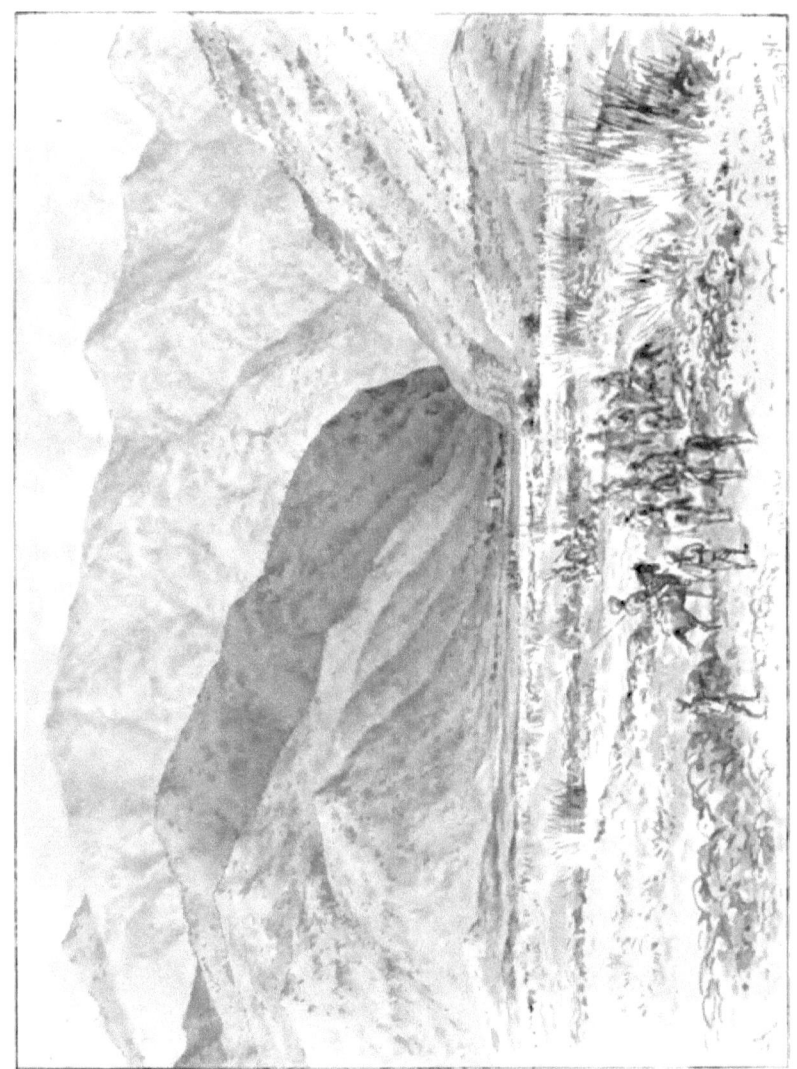

THE APPROACH TO THE
SHIN DURRA GORGE.

THE JAROBI VILLAGES.

The Shin Durra proved to be a long winding glen, which became wilder and narrower as it penetrated the hills, with steep cliffs on either side. About four miles from the mouth it opened out, and a cluster of villages was found on the spurs and hillsides, one large one, called Tola Killa, being on a hillock in the bed of the nullah. Two companies of the 20th Punjab Infantry were pushed on, as Jarobi was said to be beyond these villages. The Staff and No. 3 Mountain Battery with a small escort remained near Tola Killa, and a heavy thunderstorm with pouring rain came on about 2 p.m. Small groups of the enemy were seen high up on the hills.

THE JAROBI VILLAGES IN THE SHIN DURRA. THE STAFF AND No. 3 MOUNTAIN BATTERY IN A RAINSTORM, SEPTEMBER 25TH.

THE FIGHT AT THE HADDA MULLAH'S MOSQUE.

A SHORT distance beyond Tola Killa was a "jumat" or mosque, with a few mud hovels enclosed by a small wall. This was "Jarobi" proper, and the home of the Hadda Mullah. The leading party of the 20th Punjab Infantry who entered the enclosure were at once attacked by some seven or eight swordsmen, who were killed after a hand-to-hand fight, in which the Native officer with the party behaved with great gallantry, killing two men with his own hand. At the same time a hot fire was opened from the rocks and bushes on the small Kotal behind the mosque, and also from a sangar in front of a little village high up on the cliff above. Some of the Gurkhas came up as a reinforcement, but as the day was drawing on Genl. Elles ordered a retirement, and the 28th Bombay Pioneers covered the retreat, which was carried out after the villages had been burned. There were about 25 casualties all told, divided between the 20th Punjab Infantry, Sappers and 28th Pioneers, one or two men being wounded mortally. The enemy followed up for about a mile, and "sniped" our camp freely during the night.

THE FIGHT AT THE HADDA
MULLAH'S MOSQUE AT JAROBI,
SEPTEMBER 25TH.

MANZIRI CHINA.

The force now proceeded to "walk round" the Bohai Dag, destroying all refractory villages whose maliks refused to come to terms. Manziri China was one of these, and was blown up and burnt on the 26th September.

MANZIRI CHINA. TROOPS DESTROYING REFRACTORY VILLAGES, SEPTEMBER 26TH.

THE BOHAI DAG AND AFGHAN FRONTIER, NEAR MANZIRI CHINA.

At the head of the Bohai Dag is a low pass into Afghan territory, among bare rocky hills, marked in the official map as the Jalala Pass, but known locally as Manziri China, being near the village of that name.

The 20th Punjab Infantry are the regiment in the sketch, under Colonel Woon.

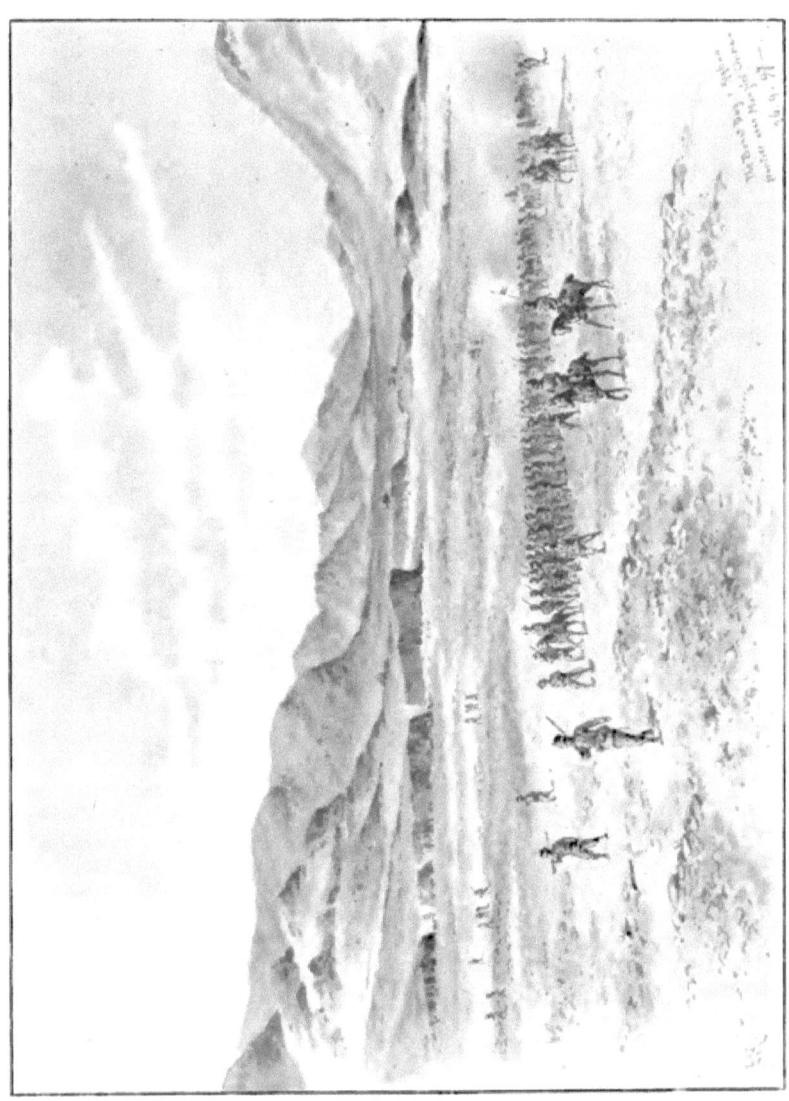

BRIG.-GENERAL WESTMACOTT,
C.B., D.S.O., COMMANDING
1st BRIGADE, MOHMAND
FIELD FORCE.

Mr. MERK, C.S.I.,
CHIEF POLITICAL OFFICER,
MOHMAND FIELD FORCE.

DESTROYING THE KHUDA KHEL VILLAGES.

A REFRACTORY collection of villages belonging to the Khuda Khel (a section of the Mohmands) was dealt with on the 27th, and a skirmish with the inhabitants ensued. A good deal of firing went on from the cliffs overlooking the villages while they were being destroyed, and the Bombay Mountain Battery (No. 5) shelled these heights thoroughly. The Gurkhas also climbed the spur on the right, and turned out some small parties of the enemy who occupied it.

There were some five or six casualties. On this day a man of the Somerset Light Infantry unaccountably got left behind. He apparently fell asleep somewhere, and was overlooked during the retirement. Luckily he was not found by the inhabitants, and after spending the night in a cave, rejoined the force the next day some 10 miles off, after having been given up as lost.

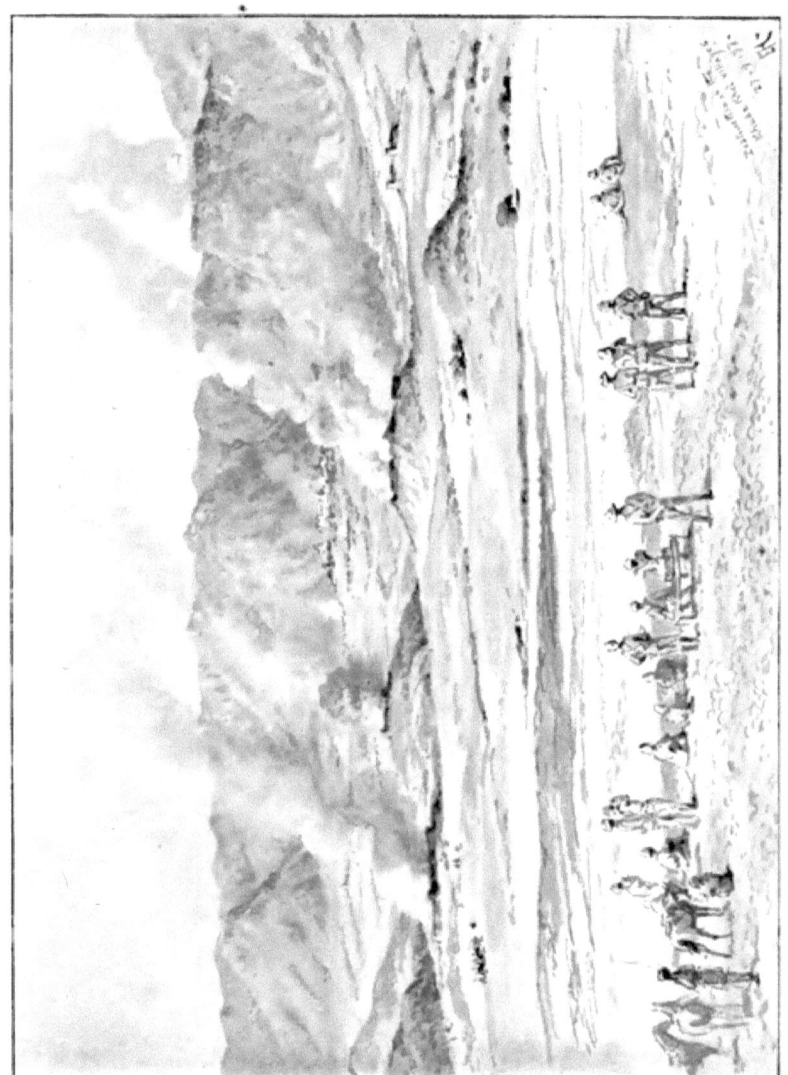

DESTROYING THE KHUDA KHEL VILLAGES, SEPTEMBER 27TH.

THE SAMGHAKHEI PASS.

The Samghakhei Pass is the direct route from the Bohai Dag to Lalpura on the Kabul River, the chief town in the Afghan Mohmand territory.

A cavalry party reconnoitred this, and were fired on from the village near, which was supposed to be "friendly," the Malik having come to terms the day previous. A battalion and a battery were sent across at once, and waited for some hours in a hot sun, while negotiations and explanations were proceeding. Eventually the sniping was stated to be "all a mistake," and the reconnaissance was completed without further incident. On arriving at Nahaki, I heard that Genl. Meiklejohn and his Staff were *not* to go to Tirah after all, so on receipt of the telegram, hastened back with all speed viâ Shubkudder, Peshawur, and the Malakand to Bajour, rejoining my Brigade at Inayat Killa on the 7th October.

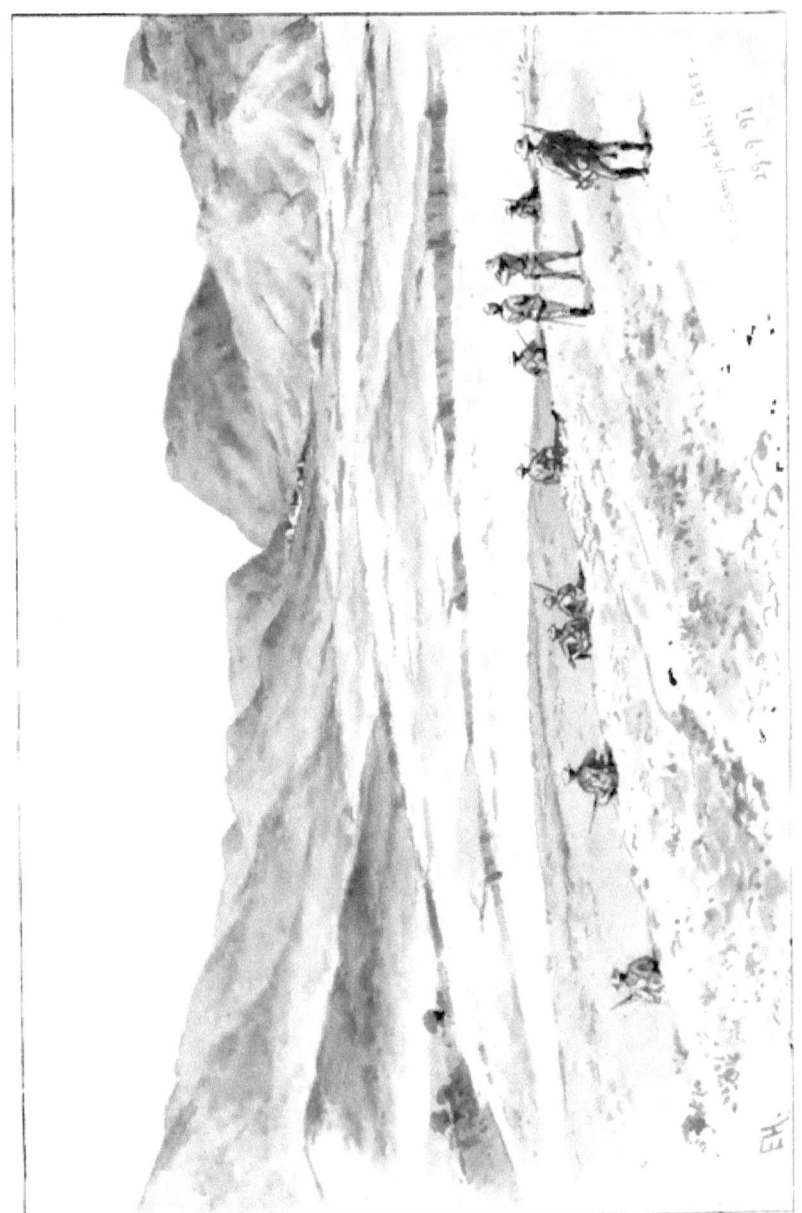

THE SAMGHAKHEI PASS.

BRIG.-GENERAL MACGREGOR,
D.S.O., COMMANDING
2ND BRIGADE, MOHMAND
FIELD FORCE.

KEY TO PHOTOGRAPH OF GENERAL OFFICER COMMANDING 2nd BRIGADE MOHMAND FIELD FORCE AND HIS STAFF, WITH OFFICERS OF THE 1st REGIMENT PATIALA SIKHS, IMPERIAL SERVICE TROOPS.

In the *front row* (sitting) are the four Subadars, or Company Commanders.

In the *2nd row* (sitting), commencing from the left, are Lt. Tytler (Gordon Highlanders), Transport Officer; Capt. Hudson, D.A.Q.M.G.; Brig.-Genl. Macgregor; Capt. Cox, Inspecting Officer (I.G.T.); and Lt. Davidson, Asst. Ins. Officer.

In the *3rd row* (standing) are Lt. Drake-Brockman, Coms: Officer; Lt. E. Ridgeway, Orderly Officer; Major Singh, Lt.-Col. Sunda Singh, Adjutant Ruttem Singh, and Asst. Surgeon.

BRIG.-GENERAL MACGREGOR AND STAFF, WITH
OFFICERS OF THE 1st REGIMENT PATIALA SIKHS.
PHOTOGRAPH TAKEN ON THE KABUL RIVER, IN THE
MOHMAND EXPEDITION, SEPTEMBER, 1897.

BAJOUR ONCE MORE.

AMONG THE MAMUNDS AND SALARZAIS.

STAFF OF THE 2ND BRIGADE, MALAKAND FIELD FORCE.

INAYAT KILLA.

INAYAT KILLA is at the entrance of a wide spreading valley in Bajour, at the head of which is a range of high hills forming the boundary between Bajour and Asmar.

Genl. Jeffreys' severe fighting on the 16th September took place at the eastern end of the valley, among the hills shown in the sketch, on the top of which Capt. Ryder's company of the 35th Sikhs was cut off and suffered heavily. Genl. Jeffreys himself spent the night with No. 8 Bengal Mountain Battery and a few Sappers and Infantry, in a small village called Balot, shown just over the right hand tower of the fort in the sketch.

My Brigade had reached Inayat Killa a couple of days previous to my arrival, but all fighting was over, and negotiations with the tribesmen were already going on, so I did not miss much.

INAYAT KILLA AND THE EASTERN
END OF THE MAMUND VALLEY.

ARRANGING TERMS OF PEACE WITH THE MAMUND JIRGAHS.

On the 12th October, the Jirgahs, or representative councils of the Mamunds, came into camp, and a durbar was held, at which Sir Bindon Blood and Major Deane, our Chief Political Officer, arranged the terms of peace with them.

Rahim Shah, Major Deane's native assistant, made a speech, explaining to the assembled elders the conditions proposed; such as surrender of all captured rifles, money fines, &c., and after a short discussion the spokesman of the Mamunds signified their acceptance of the terms, and the Staff returned to camp.

SIR BINDON BLOOD.
MAJOR DEANE.

NAWAGAI'S
HEIR APPARENT.

SPOKESMAN (MAMUND).

DURBAR WITH THE MAMUND
JIRGAHS AT INAYAT KILLA,
OCTOBER 12TH.

KHAN OF KHAR.
KHAN OF JHAR.
KHAN OF NAWAGAI.
NAWAGAI'S SON

151

MAJOR DEANE, C.S.I.,
CHIEF POLITICAL OFFICER,
MALAKAND FIELD FORCE.

MATASHAH.

AFTER settling with the Mamunds, the 1st and 2nd Brigades moved into the Salarzai country, and remained in camp at Matashah from the 14th till the 20th October, while our politicals were treating with the clans. Some sections of the tribe took a deal of persuading, and used to come and "snipe" into camp regularly every night.

SALARZAI VALLEY, BAJOUR, FROM THE 10TH FIELD BATTERY CAMP AT MATASHAH.

PASHAT.

To assist the Salarzai elders in coming to a decision, a demonstration in force was made on the 16th, and a strong column marched up the valley to Pashat, the chief town of the Salarzais. The 10th Field Battery accompanied this force, and certainly no field artillery ever penetrated so far into the hills before.

A curious incident occurred during the day. A Salarzai addressed our troops in very good "nigger English," and it was found that he had spent ten years in Demerara on a sugar plantation. This worthy answered to the name of "Jabez," and was inclined to be very friendly.

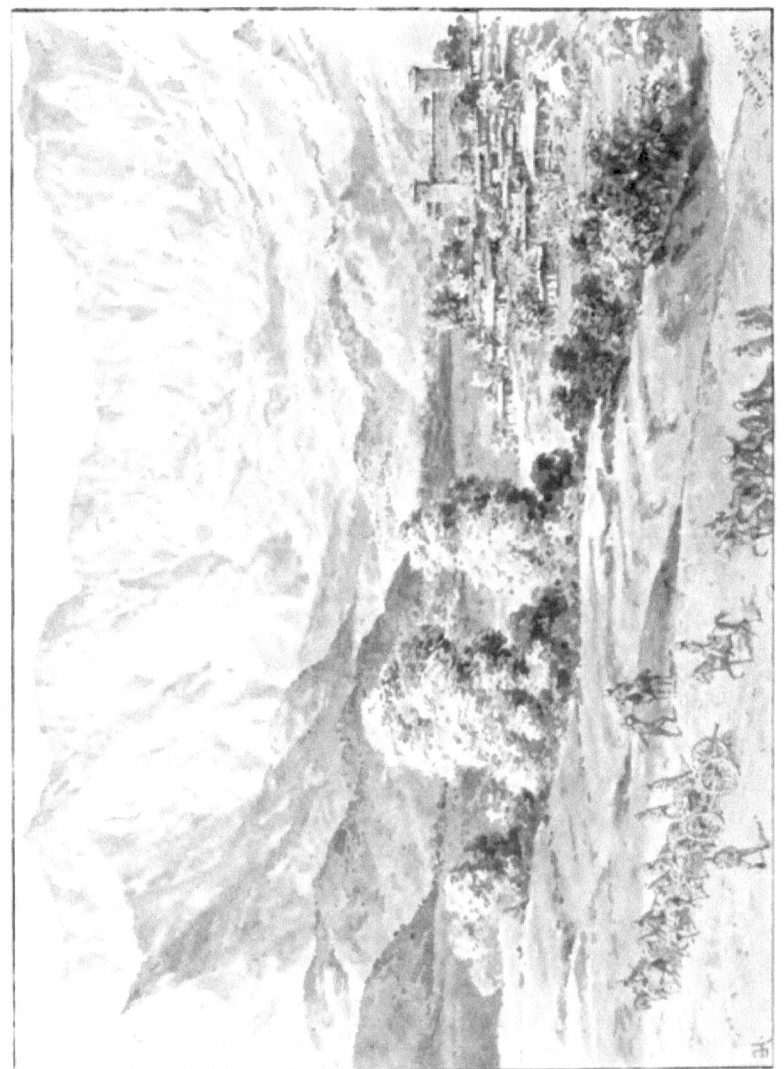

PASHAT, IN THE SALARZAI VALLEY.
10TH FIELD BATTERY ON THE MARCH.

FORDING THE PANJKORA.

Eventually the Salarzais, Shamozais, and various other clans were all settled with by the politicals, without the necessity for coercion by the troops ; and we proceeded to retrace our steps along the now well-known route to the Panjkora—and so on to the Malakand.

The Panjkora bridge was reported to be unsafe for camel traffic, so all mules were sent by the bridge, and our camel transport crossed the river by a ford which was also used by the Guides Cavalry. One or two camels were lost, as the stream, though not very deep, was very swift, and if a camel fell with his load he was quickly washed into deep water and drowned.

The spur of the hill on the left of the sketch was the scene of the Guides' fight in 1895, and Colonel Battye was killed near the tree at the foot of the slope.

GUIDES CAVALRY AND CAMEL TRANSPORT FORDING THE PANJKORA.

www.ingramcontent.com/pod-product-compliance
Lightning Source LLC
Chambersburg PA
CBHW030311170426
43202CB00009B/966